Anthem II
Let thy hand be strengthened
No. 1

FOUR CORONATION ANTHEMS

G. F. HANDEL

Anthem I
Zadok the priest

No. 2

No. 3

Anthem III
The King shall rejoice
No. 1

No. 2

* Throughout this movement, both ♪♪ and ♪.♪ may be performed ♪³♪.

No. 3

No. 4

Anthem IV
My heart is inditing
No. 1

No. 2

No. 3

No. 4

Reproduced and printed by Halstan & Co. Ltd., Amersham, Bucks., England

ISBN 978-0-19-335271-1

OXFORD UNIVERSITY PRESS

9 780193 352711